MW01264194

CPR & CPR[+]
How Caring, Praying, and Reaching Out
Can Bless and Develop Others

CPR & CPR⁺

How **C**aring, **P**raying, and **R**eaching Out Can Bless and Develop Others

Rick Mann, PhD

CPR & CPR⁺
How Caring, Praying, and Reaching Out Can Bless and Develop Others
By Rick Mann, PhD

Published by: ClarionStrategy LLC, Nashville, TN
www.ClarionStrategy.com

Copyright © 2024 Rick Mann

All Rights Reserved

Dedication

To all those who aspire to bless more people more
and to those who want to mobilize Christ followers
to advance the Kingdom of God.

TABLE OF CONTENTS

**Clarion**Life Series

Living and Leading Intentionally: 31 Tools for Multiplying Christ-centered, Spirit-filled, Healthy Strategic Leaders by Rick Mann, PhD, and Rob Douglas, DMin (Coming later in 2024)

Becoming Multiplying Ministry Leaders Who Multiply Leaders: Lessons from Jesus, Barnabas, and Paul by Rick Mann, PhD (Coming in late 2024)

ACKNOWLEDGMENTS

Thanks to Tony, Chris, Steve, and John, who prompted discussions about caring, praying, and reaching out to others.

Thanks to Dr. Rob Douglas and all the churches and leaders who have embraced CPR in the Central Pacific District of the Christian and Missionary Alliance.

Last but not least, I offer thanks to my dear wife, Cheri, who has championed my life and leadership over so many decades. Without her prayers and loyalty, none of this would have happened.

Preface

"When he saw the crowds, he had compassion on
them because they were harassed and helpless,
like sheep without a shepherd."

–Mt 9:36

Most days, Cheri and I spend some time in prayer together. When we pray, you will often hear us say, "Lord, help us to bless more people more today." We believe that we are on an adventurous mission with Jesus, and we look forward to what he is going to do in us and through us each day.

When it comes to blessing more people more, we can reach into Genesis 12, where we read that God chose Abraham and raised him up to bless the nations.

"Go from your country, your people and your father's household to the land I will show you. I will make you into a great nation, and I will bless you...and all peoples on earth will be blessed through you."

This is our prayer for both us and you.

OVERVIEW

CPR was birthed out of a conversation I had with several participants in a men's small group at my church. I asked the leaders if they could "pastor" the group. They said, "Yes, we can, but we don't like the word 'pastor' because we are not pastors."

"Okay," I responded, "Could you care, pray, and reach out to the guys in this group?"

They agreed, "Yes."

I said, "Okay, then let's just call it CPR."

We then presented the CPR concepts to the men's group, and they have moved it forward. The purpose of CPR is to bless more people more. Blessing more people more has two connotations. First, it means more people quantitatively. Instead of blessing 100 people, let's try to bless 1,000 people. It also has a qualitative connotation. Instead of just blessing each person in simple ways, let's seek to bless them in deeper ways. As we will discuss later, there are so many lonely and uncared for people in our world. This is one way we can all bless more people more.

CPR+ is an extension of CPR with the purpose of developing the people around you. Most churches need more active and engaged people at all levels. This is one way to get there from here. CPR and CPR+ can be done by anyone and from anywhere. While CPR is targeted toward everyday people, CPR+ is more focused on developing people and leaders in your church and in the wider world.

CLARIONLIFE SERIES

The purpose of ClarionLife books is to help readers develop their spiritual and strategic lives and leadership. In a word, it is about being more intentional. These books are designed with the following features in mind:

- Can be read in an evening or weekend.
- Serve as a practical guide for getting started.
- Easy for nonacademic people to understand.
- Balance spiritual and strategic development.

In a word, it is about being more intentional.

No matter where you are in your life or leadership journey, I hope that these tools can be of benefit to you.

NOTE: The Clarion banner also includes the ClarionStrategy Tool-Box series of books. These books are designed to help practical and tactical people be more strategic in their personal, professional, and organizational lives. All of the Clarion titles can be found on Amazon.

THE WHY, HOW, AND WHAT FRAMEWORK

In both the ClarionStrategy ToolBox and ClarionLife series, I draw on some of the material from the Golden Circle model popularized by Simon Sinek, the author of *Start With Why* (2011). As of 2023, Sinek's TED talk on the Golden Circle was the 4th most-watched TED talk and counts over 63 million views. In his work, Sinek talks about three circles: **Why, How,** and **What.** He expounds on **why** companies do what they do. He then discusses **how** companies do what they do. Lastly, he talks about **what** companies do. I have adapted this thinking to this work here, following the same outline for each of the tools listed in this book.

WHY It Matters – First, we look at why the concept or tool matters. This includes the importance of understanding the concepts and putting them into practice.

HOW It Works – Next, we unpack the main concepts that are central to the particular tool.

WHAT To Do Next? – Lastly, I suggest how you can put the tool to use in your life and leadership.

This simple "why, how, and what" framework can help you learn and apply each tool more quickly.

NOTE: The CPR and CPR⁺ tools discussed in this book can be easily adapted for the workplace. Many emerging leaders under 40 are looking for leaders who will care for them *and* help them grow and develop. You can be that leader.

How to Use This Book

*"The harvest is **plentiful,** but the workers are **few.**
Ask the Lord of the harvest, therefore, to **send out
workers** into his harvest."*

–Mt 9:37-38

According to the verse above, there is nothing wrong with the harvest. The harvest is plentiful. The problem is the shortage of workers for the harvest. This book seeks to address this problem. It is designed to be used by two groups of people: everyday Christian folks and those seeking to multiply Christian workers and leaders.

EVERYDAY CHRISTIAN FOLKS

The CPR portion of this book is designed for every child, teen, man, and woman in our local churches. You may wonder if 5-year-olds can do CPR. I think they can and certainly 10- and 15-year-olds can. All of us can use this simple tool to bless more people more all around us.

These CPR materials will provide you with what you need to engage the harvest around you. Yes, you can be a worker in the harvest no matter where you are.

LEADERS MULTIPLYING LEADERS

The CPR⁺ portion of this book is designed for those who are seeking to develop and multiply workers and leaders around them. For example, you could teach CPR to your youth or adult small group. On an individual level, you could sit down with someone and use the tools from CPR⁺. By putting the CPR tools into their hands and lives, you can help move them toward greater kingdom harvest.

USE AS AN INDIVIDUAL AND/OR SMALL GROUP GUIDE

As a Guide for Your Own Use: You can use this CPR guide for your own personal life and leadership as you care, pray, and reach out to people in your world. You can also use the CPR⁺ tools to develop workers and leaders. Lastly, you can adapt CPR and CPR⁺ tools for leading teams at work.

As a Guide for Working With Others: You can give a copy of this book to a Christian friend and then meet with them each month to go over it together.

For Small Groups: You can also use this book as a guide for a small group. It works best when you use it for 10 or more weeks, although you can also condense it to work in 5-7 weeks.

You could use the following pitch to start a CPR small group at your church:

> If you would like to bless more people more in your neighborhood, church, workplace, or school, join us for our CPR group. We will equip people to care, pray, and reach out to those around them. This group will be both practical and interactive.

NOTE: The principles discussed in this book apply equally to adults and teens. Therefore, don't hesitate to use it with a youth group.

Here is an example of how you could use this book in a 10-week small group format:

1. Intro to CPR
2. Caring
3. Praying
4. Reaching Out
5. Next CPR Steps
6. Intro to CPR[+]
7. Caring[+]
8. Praying[+]
9. Reaching Out[+]
10. Next CPR[+] Steps

Buying in bulk. You can buy this book on Amazon for $8.99 plus shipping. You can also buy in bulk for $5 per copy. This includes shipping costs ($50 for 10 books delivered). For bulk orders, just email Info@ClarionLife.org or call 615-268-0596. Allow 3-4 weeks to receive bulk orders.

CPR

BLESSING
MORE PEOPLE
MORE

Introduction to CPR

*"The surgeon general of the United States recently named loneliness as **America's top health problem**, revealing that nearly half of the country's adults report feelings of isolation and deteriorating mental health."*

–Aaron Damiani, "Take a Risk and Make a Friend"
Christianity Today, September 11, 2023

In 2021, on an October day in Northeast Ohio, Steve Raichilson was playing tennis with a friend when his friend collapsed. Having been trained in CPR, but having never done this before, Steve performed CPR on his friend and after what seemed like an hour, and the arrival of some EMTs, his friend was revived. We all need good friends like Steve. Unfortunately, most Americans don't have that many friends. In the church, we would hope it would be better, but often it is not. We gather together regularly, but we may not connect, care, pray, or reach out to one another.

Let me ask you a question. How many people do you have in your life who 1) Care for you, 2) Pray for you, and 3) Reach out to you each month? I refer to such people as "CPR friends." A CPR friend is someone who cares for you, prays for you, and reaches out to you. We all need some friends who do these things regularly. In this book, we will discuss how you can be a CPR friend.

> *A CPR friend is someone who cares for you,*
> *prays for you, and reaches out to you.*

We Live in a Lonely World

In the U.S., we are experiencing an epidemic of loneliness. According to pre-pandemic reporting by Elena Renken of NPR, "more than three in five Americans are lonely, with more and more people reporting feeling like they are left out, poorly understood and lacking companionship" (2020). As a part of the Making Caring Common project at Harvard, the university published a report entitled: "Loneliness in America: How the Pandemic Has Deepened an Epidemic of Loneliness and What We Can Do About It."

> *In the U.S., we are experiencing*
> *an epidemic of loneliness.*

This report touches on how our Christian tradition placed importance on caring for others.

> We need to return to an idea that was central to our founding and is at the heart of many great religious traditions: We have commitments to ourselves, but we also have vital commitments to each other, including to those who are vulnerable (2021).

When we look at the Book of Matthew, we read these words about Jesus:

When he saw the crowds, he had compassion on them, because they were harassed and helpless like sheep without a shepherd.

Mt 9:36

We are seeking the heart of Jesus here. We can take on his heart. As we take on the heart of Jesus, we can be mobilized to care for those in our church and in our community.

Unleashing the Church

The Harvard report makes three recommendations: One of them is "[To build] not just our physical but our social infrastructure at every level of government..." I am not sure the government can make a major impact on the issue of loneliness in America. What I do know is that when the church is equipped and unleashed, caring can happen all over the place. When we take on the heart of Jesus, we too can have compassion on the crowds around us.

You Can Do This

You may feel a little unsure of yourself in talking with others about spiritual things. This is way easier. Our goal is to bless more people more. This is not complicated, and this is not hard. You can do this!

Our goal is to bless more people more.

A One-Foot Fence

In my coaching book, *Coaching: The First Five Tools for Strategic Leaders,* I talk about the one-foot fence. A one-foot fence is not hard to cross. All it takes is a bit of willingness. CPR is a one-foot fence. Keep the following in mind:

- The goal is to bless more people more through caring, praying, and reaching out.
- We can all be a CPR friend to someone.
- If you don't want to, you don't even have to talk much to care, pray, and reach out (you can text them).
- Partner with some other CPR folks so you can find some encouragement and support as you seek to bless more people more.

Remember, you can do this!

Case Study with Chris

To make things a little more practical in this book, we are going to walk through a case study with Chris. Chris could be a man, woman, or even a child or teen. We will imagine that you are a small group leader at your church and that Chris is in your group. The group you lead might be for children, youth, or adults. It could also be a ministry team such as worship, facilities, etc.

Application for Individuals

1. Where do you experience lonely people in your world?
2. When you see the crowds, do you have compassion or are you irritated?
3. Who is a lonely person in your world you could bless?
4. Are you more of an introvert or an extrovert?
5. Do you have a friend who each month cares for you, prays for you, and reaches out to you?

Application for Small Groups

1. Who in your group is trained in medical CPR?
2. Not using their real name, share about a lonely person in your world with your group.

3. How do you feel about talking with others about spiritual topics?
4. How comfortable would you be caring for, praying for, and reaching out to someone?
5. Why do so many people feel lonely even though they know a lot of people?

CARING

When he saw the crowds, he had compassion on them, because they were harassed and helpless, like sheep without a shepherd.

–Mt 9:36

When you care about someone, you hope the best for them. You support them and you help them as you can in times of need. Caring for others was at the center of Jesus' life and ministry. In the Gospels, we read about Jesus' friend, Lazarus. When Lazarus died, we have that famous shortest verse in the King James Bible, "Jesus wept." Jesus cared about his friend.

You can care for your friends by demonstrating empathy and compassion, feeling with them the things they are going through. This is getting excited when they are excited and feeling their pain when they are down. You can be that CPR friend. This doesn't mean that you need to make 5-10 new best friends. Nor does it mean that you need to sacrifice all your free time. You can be a good CPR friend without spending hours each month.

WHY IT MATTERS

God cares for us and calls us to care for others. In his book on the Trinity, Darrell Johnson (2021) writes, "At the center of the universe is a relationship." God the Father, God the Son, and God the Holy Spirit invites us into a relationship. We were made for relationships. In the famous Harvard Happiness Study that has been going on for more than 85 years, the researchers' number one finding is that happiness is about the quality of our relationships. It is not about fame or fortune, power or prestige. It is about relationships.

The researchers' number one finding is that happiness is about the quality of our relationships.

Despite these realities, many, many people are lonely. As I was writing this book, I spoke with someone who told me that ever since their mother died a couple of years ago, they don't have a friend in the world. Sadly, the person said that they could go home from work on Friday and die and no one would even know about it for a week.

The good news is that we can do something about it. When that person told me that they don't have a friend in the world, I said, "You do now. I will be your friend." You can be that friend who cares.

HOW IT WORKS

Building relationships takes intentionality. In the earlier introduction to this book, I quoted from a *Christianity Today* article entitled: "Take a Risk and Make a Friend." The full title is "Take a Risk and Make a Friend: With God's Help, a Little Intentionality Can Go a Long Way Toward Healing Our Loneliness." Relationships take intentionality and that intentionality starts with caring.

A few years ago, I came across some research that claimed that American men don't have five friends. I went through my mental list of people I know. I could come up with five friends, but it was a little harder than I would have thought. I began to talk with my friends about this and a number admitted they didn't have five friends. Between us, we know hundreds of people, but we all realized that having friends and building relationships takes intentionality. CPR is a great on-ramp for new relationships. It doesn't take a lot of time and you can bless more people more.

Blessing More People More

Because so many people do not have people who care about them, this is an opportunity for you to bless them with your care. For example, when I go out to eat, I will say to the wait staff person, "When our food comes, we are going to pray for our food and wondered how we could pray for you. Do you have any needs with your family, your finances, your health, or work that we could pray for?" I have done this hundreds of times and they will usually come up with something. More importantly, they know I care. Many people who work in restaurants lead hard lives. Some are divorced, single parents and are working at night because they must. Also, many wait staff get yelled at every day. When we stop and care, it blesses them. It may be the only caring human connection they have all day.

Just this week, Cheri and I went out to eat at Ruby Tuesday. Our waiter was a strong-looking 40-year-old guy. When we asked him how we could pray for him, he immediately started crying and couldn't stop. He apologized for his tears. When we said that we are all good, he said, "It is just so rare for people to ask how I am doing. It caught me off guard."

Very Draining People (VDP)

We all probably have people in our lives that are very draining. We can call these people "Very Draining People," or VDPs. I know it doesn't sound nice to say it that way, but it is the reality for many of us.

The question is not whether you have VDPs in your life, it is how you manage them. Let's say that one of your VDPs is your adult brother. Maybe he is critical of you and others and is negative about almost everything. First, you can't control him or what he does. You can only control what you do. In Matthew 5:43-45, Jesus says:

You have heard that it was said, "You shall love your neighbor and hate your enemy." But I say to you, Love your enemies and pray for those who persecute you, so that you may be sons of your Father who is in heaven.

You can care for this person even if they are not pleasant. It is a matter of figuring out how you can bless him while minimizing the harm he does to you.

WHAT TO DO NEXT

Take time to do some self-reflection. Where are you at with your portfolio of relationships? How would you describe your network of relationships? Here are some diagnostic questions:

1. How many friends would you say you have who 1) Care for you, 2) Pray for you, and 3) Reach out to you each month? If you don't have a long list, you are like most people.
2. Do you put more into your network of relationships than you get out of them? If so, this is more common than we often think.
3. How many toxic or VDP people do you have in your life? Can you bless them and keep them from harming you?
4. Who are 3-5 people in your church or community that you could care for?
5. What are some next steps you could take to bless more people more?

Case Study with Chris

Chris is in your life group and has been coming regularly. Maybe in your group training, they talked about CPR. An easy place to start doing CPR is with people in your group. There could be several reasons that you choose Chris to be on your CPR list.

- You seem to have a good connection with them.
- When you prayed, the Lord brought them to mind.
- Chris has been a little more engaged than some of the others.

You can get started by being a bit more intentional about caring for Chris. This can be as simple as saying "hi" or saying that you are glad they come to the group.

Application for Individuals

1. Who are people in your life who care about you?
2. Do you have any very draining people (VDP) in your life?
3. Pray and reflect and ask God who he might have you care for.
4. How full is your relational plate?

Application for Small Groups

1. Share with those in your group about where you are at concerning those who care for you.
2. Where do you feel you are at emotionally when it comes to caring for others?
3. Could this group care for the people in this group?

PRAYING

For this reason, since the day we heard about you,
we have not stopped praying for you.
We continually ask God to fill you with
the knowledge of his will through all the wisdom
and understanding that the Spirit gives.

–Colossians 1:9

Caring for a friend can lead to praying for them. Many times, in the New Testament, we are called to pray for one another. In Colossians 1:9 above, we read, "For this reason, since the day we heard about you, we have not stopped praying for you." If you know what the people around you are facing, you can better pray for them on those issues. Even if you don't know what they are going through, you can still pray the Scriptures into their life. Later in this verse, we also read, "asking that you may be filled with the knowledge of his will in all spiritual wisdom and understanding." You can pray this prayer for anyone.

God invites us to pray for one another. The impact can be significant. In the Lord's Prayer, we read:

"Thy kingdom come;
thy will be done on earth as it is in heaven."

When we pray for someone, we can help them experience a touch of heaven here on earth. Let's say I pray for Sue that she can experience God's peace and rest in her heart and soul.

Yes, our prayers can change things. I like the five words that author Rob Reimer uses in his book, *Spiritual Authority* (2020): "Touch heaven and change earth." You can be that CPR friend who touches heaven on behalf of someone on earth.

WHY IT MATTERS

If we want to bless more people more, we can do something about it. We can pray for people and see their lives changed. This is so easy because you don't even need to talk with them. I talked about CPR in a church and later the pastor told me about one of their teens who came and spoke with him. The teen said, "I can do this. Even though I am introvert, I can do this!" If I am driving down the road and someone in front of me starts going into road rage, I can pray for them right then and God can touch their lives in the moment. Again and again, Jesus talked about how the Kingdom of God is coming. While the fullness of kingdom will not be present in this age, God invites us to pray:

Thy kingdom come;
thy will be done on earth as it is in heaven.

Let's join in with these five words: Touch heaven and change earth. Praying for people is a spiritual activity that invites the power of the Holy Spirit to come and touch the lives of people. Don't be surprised if even supernatural things happen. We can pray for the healing of hearts and bodies and see God divinely touch them in amazing ways. Yes, you can be that CPR friend who touches heaven and changes the world around you.

HOW IT WORKS

There are lots of ways to pray for people. Here are a few:

- We can pray for people from the **Scriptures**. See the Appendix of this book for some example prayers.
- We can **ask people** how we can pray for them and then pray in accordance with this.
- We can pray and **ask God** how we should pray for this person.
- We can join with others in praying for people.

Let's unpack each of these.

Praying for People from the Scriptures

If you don't have any specific prayer requests from those you are caring for, there are many prayers you can use from the Scriptures. Let's start with some scriptural prayers for Christians you know and then we will look at some scriptural prayers you can pray for those who have yet to meet Christ.

Scriptural Prayers for Christians:

- Romans 15:3: "May the God of hope fill you with all joy and peace as you trust in him, so that you may overflow with hope by the power of the Holy Spirit."
- Ephesians 1:17: "...keep asking that the God of our Lord Jesus Christ, the glorious Father, may give you the Spirit of wisdom and revelation, so that you may know him better."
- 1 Thessalonians 3:12: "May the Lord make your love increase and overflow for each other and for everyone else."

These are prayers you can pray for any Christian you know.

Scriptural Prayers for Those Who Have Yet to Meet Christ

- Psalm 23: "He makes me lie down in green pastures, he leads me beside quiet waters, he refreshes my soul. He guides me along the right paths for his name's sake. Even though I walk through the darkest valley, I will fear no evil, for you are with me; your rod and your staff, they comfort me.
- Acts 16:14: "The Lord opened her heart to respond to Paul's message."
- Acts 26:18 (NLT): "Open their eyes, so they may turn from darkness to light and from the power of Satan to God."
- 2 Corinthians 10:4 (NLT): "We use God's mighty weapons, not worldly weapons, to knock down the strongholds of human reasoning and to destroy false arguments. We destroy every proud obstacle that keeps people from knowing God."
- Genesis 12: "And all peoples on earth will be blessed through you."

These are wonderful prayers that you can pray for anyone who has yet to meet Christ. You may want to memorize some of these passages so you can use them to pray anywhere at any time. Again, in the Appendix of this book, there are many other scriptural prayers that you can pray for others.

At Restaurants: "How Can I Pray for You?"

Earlier, I mentioned how you can pray for people at restaurants. This year, I had this conversation with a lady who was serving our table. We continued with short interchanges as she came back and forth. After about a half hour, she came back to our table and asked, "Could I give you another prayer request? Could you pray that my husband could find a job?" Time and time again at restaurants, we can bless more people more.

In everyday settings, I often ask, "How can I be praying for you this month?" People usually have some things to share. Because I don't have a great memory, I try to write their prayer requests down.

Praying for Them Right There

It is common for Christians to say they will pray for others as needs arise. Sometimes we forget to do just that. Therefore, if the setting seems reasonable, I will ask them if I can pray for them right then and there. Most weeks at Trevecca where I teach, I interview applicants to our doctoral program. At the end of those interviews, I will often add, "Before I let you go today, can I pray for you?" This process can be used in all kinds of situations. It is one more way to care and pray for people.

Praying Is a Divine Adventure

As mentioned before, praying for people is a spiritual activity that connects God in heaven with people on earth. Sometimes, God will bring something to mind to pray about for a person that I didn't even know. Take time to pause and ask the Holy Spirit to show you how you can pray for others. Be open to what may come to mind that you didn't know or hadn't expected.

When we are at a loss as to how to pray, we read in Romans 8:26-27 that the Holy Spirit is our helper:

> In the same way, the Spirit helps us in our weakness. We do not know what we ought to pray for, but the Spirit himself intercedes for us through wordless groans. And he who searches our hearts knows the mind of the Spirit, because the Spirit intercedes for God's people in accordance with the will of God.

Keeping Track of Prayer Requests

It doesn't take very long before you may forget who said what. Therefore, it often works best to write down the who, the what, and the when in the form of the name, prayer need, and date. You can do this in a paper notebook, on your phone, or on a computer. In the Appendix of this book, there is a template of a blank form I use so that I don't forget how to pray for people going forward.

Following Up With Prayer Requests

If I can, I try to circle back in a week or two (or three) to let them know I have been praying for them and to see whether there are any updates. Again, this does not have to be intense. Just keep things natural in the flow of everyday conversations.

Confidentiality Is Critical

One Sunday, I was talking with a pastor and I asked him how I could be praying for him. Although I didn't know him that well, he quickly shared some very personal things. The only way this relationship works is if I keep **lock tight confidentiality.** When you get prayer requests from others, make sure you keep those requests confidential and safe. If you write them down in a notebook or other place where they could potentially be seen by others, use a pseudonym or another strategy so that they can remain anonymous should you lose your notebook.

WHAT TO DO NEXT

As you begin to pray for others, there are several things you will want to work through. Here are a few topics to address:

- **Your pacing of prayer:** You can pray for people each day, week, or month. You can also pray for people as they come to mind. At a minimum, I work on praying for my CPR friends at least once a month.
- **Scriptural prayers, their requests, or as the Lord leads:** You can pray for people using scriptural prayers. Again, there are sample prayers in the Appendix of this book. You can use the prayer requests that people give you. Lastly, you can just pray the prayers that come to mind.

- **Alone or with them:** You can pray for people when you are alone. You can also pray with them if you are comfortable praying out loud with others and it seems appropriate at the time.

There is no right answer to these topics. How you pray for others will be different from how someone else prays for people. Just try to find a practice that fits you well and blesses others.

Find an Accountability Partner

We are all busy, and it's easy to get lost in the shuffle. I suggest that you find a CPR accountability partner that you can touch base with each month. This person can help you to stay on track. This is not about pressure or guilt; it is just about ensuring that you follow through on what you care about. If you work with others to stay accountable, just remember that all your prayers for others need to remain confidential.

Case Study with Chris

In your small group this week, you broke out into pairs, and you paired up with Chris. You asked, "Chris, how can I be praying for you this month?" They said that you could pray for them concerning an issue at work and for their mother, who has not been well recently.

You could also just chat with Chris during one of the breaks and ask, "How can I be praying for you this month?"

Jot down their prayer requests somewhere so you don't forget them. You can use the form at the end of this book if you want. You might also want to get Chris's cell phone number so you can text them in the future.

Application for Individuals

1. Is praying for others new to you?
2. How do you feel praying out loud?
3. Are you more inclined to pray scriptural prayers or to pray for others as the Lord leads?

Application for Small Groups

1. Is there anyone in the group who would like to practice praying out loud?
2. Could you break into groups of 2-3 to pray for each other?
3. Without sharing any identities or requests, does anyone have something to share about how your prayers for other people have been answered?

Reaching Out

*I long to see you so that I may impart to you
some spiritual gift to make you strong—that is,
that you and I may be mutually encouraged
by each other's faith.*

–Romans 1:11-12

CPR friends are not passive. Not only do they pray for their friends, but they also reach out to them. There are lots of ways to do this. You can text them, call them, email them, visit them, or just talk with them when you run into them.

WHY IT MATTERS

Human touch is a powerful force in people's lives. When people touch us through their care, it grows our sense of well-being. Unfortunately, most of us do not have many people in our lives who intentionally reach out and touch us each month. You can be that person.

HOW IT WORKS

Just as every person is different, so too are the ways that you can reach out to others. You can find ways to reach out to others that work for you and seem appropriate at the time.

Different Ways to Reach Out

There are many ways to touch the lives of others. Here are some examples:

- Text
- Email
- Call
- Video call (FaceTime, Zoom, etc.)
- Short, in-person conversation (after church)
- Sit-down coffee
- Going for a walk together

Peoples' Preferred Touch

While I prefer talking with people on the phone, my millennial sons and daughters-in-law prefer texting. Since this is about them and not about me, I like to reach out to people using their preferred modality.

Since this is about them and not about me, I like to reach out to people using their preferred modality.

Knowing Them and Yourself

As you get to know them, you may get a feel as to the rhythms of their lives. Some people are very busy and don't need touches every week. Others live by themselves and are generally lonely. A weekly touch of some sort may be the highlight of their week.

You also need to know yourself. How much time do you have each month for reaching out? I like to look across my month and see which weeks are more open. If possible, I prefer to meet face-to-face at the beginning to hear their story. After that, shorter touches like text and emails can work well.

If you are more introverted or busier, meeting with many people, especially in-person may not work well. There is no right or wrong here, it is just a matter of knowing yourself well and knowing your CPR friends well.

Frequency

Unless you know a person well, reaching out to them several times a week can be distracting or even feel like stalking. On the other extreme, reaching out to people less than once a month can feel too distant. I find that touching people's lives at least every month is a good starting place. If you are praying for them on something that is a little more time sensitive, you may want to reach out using a time frame that seems to fit them and their situation.

Variety

Your CPR touches don't have to be the same. As we mentioned earlier, you can use a mix of texts, calls, and visits over several months.

WHAT TO DO NEXT

It is not hard to get started reaching out to others. Let's say you have a neighbor or co-worker on your CPR Friend List. Start by being intentional. Look out for them at work or in your neighborhood. When you see them, stop and talk with them. You can ask:

- "How are you doing?"
- "What's new in your world?"
- "How is your family doing?"

If you have been praying for them, you can say:

- "I have been praying for [fill in the blank here]. How are things going?"
- "You asked me to pray for your mother's surgery: how did it go?"

If you don't see them often and have their cell number, you can text them something like:

- "I was praying for you today. How are things going?
- "Any updates on your mother?"
- "How can I be praying for you this month?"

As previously mentioned, a CPR touch can take many forms. Even just a simple text can bless a friend. Remember, this touch should in some way express your care and concern.

Case Study with Chris

If you see Chris at church or in your small group, you can just mention, "Hey, I have been praying for your job and your mom. Any updates on how things are going?" If you don't run into Chris, you could text him and say, "Praying for you today, how's it going?"

Application for Individuals

- What is your preferred modality of communication?
- How long would it take you to text 5 people each month?
- What are some ways you could reach out going forward?

Application for Small Groups

- Go around the group and share with one another your preferred modality of communication.
- How much time do you have each month to reach out to people?
- Update the group on a positive exchange you have had sometime in the last month.

NEXT STEPS

Over the past three chapters, we have looked at the principles and practices of:

- Caring
- Praying
- Reaching Out

I have heard many people say, "This is so simple!" Then they also acknowledge that while it may be simple, it is meaningful and something that almost anyone can do.

WHY IT MATTERS

No tool works if you don't use it. Some experts talk about "ridiculously easy goals." What they are saying is that the hardest part of many endeavors is getting started. Before you add 10 people to your CPR list, I suggest that you start with 1-3 people. This will also help you gain some confidence and find your preferred rhythm.

HOW IT WORKS

Here are some steps you can take to get started:

- Spend some time in prayer asking the Lord who you should put on your list.
- You may want to start with one person in each category:
  - Family
  - Church person
  - Community person

What Are You Learning?

As you get started, see what you are learning. For example, when I started asking restaurant servers how I could pray for them, I would just say, "We are going to pray for our food today and wondered how we could pray for you." I noticed that people looked a little stunned, so I started adding, "Health? Family? Finances? Work? School?" People will usually pick one of those and then we are off and running. As you get some practice, you will learn more about yourself and others.

What to Do Next

Ask the Lord to show you some people today or this month that you could begin to care for and pray for. Don't overthink it. The goal is to get started blessing more people more. People will see your caring heart and will respond in kind. Recently, I was at a restaurant and asked the waitress how my wife Cheri and I could pray for her. She said that hearing that question gave her goosebumps. We had another server say, "That is so kind of you to ask." As you get some practice, you will see how positively people respond.

Case Study with Chris

You are now up and going with Chris and CPR. The goal moving forward is to be consistent month to month.

To help maintain this consistency, I like to use a CPR worksheet where you can write down prayer requests as well as monthly times of prayer and reaching out.

Application for Individuals

1. Do you feel you understand the CPR elements?
2. What are your biggest hurdles in getting started?
3. What things might keep you from moving forward?
4. Who could you start with this month?

Application for Small Groups

1. Break into groups of two or three and brainstorm who you could do CPR with.
2. Pick one person in your group who you can track with for the coming weeks as you get up and going with CPR.
3. Pray for one another that God will bless your CPR relationships as you seek to bless more people more.

CPR Friend List

The friends on your CPR list are not projects—they are just meaningful friends you want to bless. For some of you, putting this list together may be easy. It may include some friends from church or your community. Your list doesn't have to be long, and it shouldn't feel like an obligation.

Don't be afraid to add new friends to your list. Just ask the Lord who should be on your list. Whoever is on your list provides you with an opportunity to:

1. Care
2. Pray
3. Reach Out

If it seems right, you can tell the person that they are your CPR friend. If it doesn't feel right, you don't have to. There is nothing wrong with organically just caring for someone, praying for them, and reaching out to them without ever letting them know that they are one of your CPR friends.

Since I have started being a CPR friend to others, my life has been blessed and enriched. My CPR list has also helped me to maintain focus and momentum on something I care about.

You can decide whether you want to keep track of your CPR friends list in paper or digital form. In the Appendix of this book, we have included a blank CPR Friends List page that you can photocopy and use.

		J	F	M	A	M	J	J	A	S	O	N	D
Name	P												
	R												
Prayer													
Name	P												
	R												
Prayer													
Name	P												
	R												
Prayer													
Name	P												
	R												
Prayer													
Name	P												
	R												
Prayer													
Name	P												
	R												
Prayer													
Name	P												
	R												
Prayer													
Name	P												
	R												
Prayer													

CPR⁺

DEVELOPING PEOPLE, WORKERS, AND LEADERS

Introduction to CPR+

"The harvest is plentiful, but the workers are few.
Ask the Lord of the harvest, therefore,
to send out workers into his harvest field."

–Mt 9:36

CPR is a great way to bless others. These concepts can also be extended with the goal of developing the gifts and leadership of people in your world and, more specifically, your church. Each element of CPR will be extended to help others grow and develop in their leadership influence and impact.

This book highlights two realities:

1. We live in a world of lonely people.
2. There is a shortage of Christian workers and leaders both in the U.S. and overseas.

As we read in the verse above, Jesus was clear that the problem is not with the harvest. The problem is with the number of workers. In this material, we will be talking about leaders who are intentionally seeking to be used by God as a kingdom influence with those around them. These leaders could include:

- Everyday folks who work from home, go to school, or work in the community.
- Parents
- Lay leaders in local churches
- Vocational pastors and other ministry leaders who serve part-time, full-time, or bi-vocationally in ministry roles.

CPR⁺ can be used in all of these roles to help people in their world grow and develop into all that God has for them.

The problem is not with the harvest.
The problem is with the number of workers.

JESUS MINISTERED TO THE MULTITUDE AND INVESTED IN THE TWELVE

Jesus touched the lives of the multitude while at the same time he strategically invested in the twelve. In five verses found in Matthew 9 and 10 we see Jesus' strategy. Let's look at these verses:

(9:35) Jesus went through all the towns and villages, teaching in their synagogues, proclaiming the good news of the kingdom and healing every disease and sickness. (36) When he saw the crowds, he had **compassion** on them, because they were harassed and helpless, like sheep without a shepherd. (37) Then he said to his disciples, "The harvest is plentiful, but the workers are few. (38) **Ask** the Lord of the harvest, therefore, to **send out workers** into his harvest field." (10:1) Jesus called his **twelve** disciples to him and gave them **authority** to **drive** out impure spirits and to **heal** every disease and sickness. (Matthew 9:35-10:1)

In verses 35 and 36, we see that Jesus had compassion on the multitude and ministered to their many needs. Next, we see how Jesus knew it would take more workers to minister to the multitude and to extend his mission to the regions beyond. This is one of the reasons he prays to the Lord of the harvest. Lastly, Jesus commissioned the twelve disciples to go and do the same things that he was doing.

The Strategy of Jesus

In the above verses from the Book of Matthew, we see the strategy of Jesus:

1. He had compassion on the multitude.
2. He ministered to the needs of the multitude.
3. He saw the need for more workers in the harvest field.
4. He prayed for more workers.
5. He equipped and commissioned the 12 to do what he did.

These strategies are not complicated and can be used by me and you.

The Pressing Needs of the Multitude

Wherever Jesus went, he was pressed by the multitude. While he had compassion on them and touched them in so many ways, the ministry to the multitude was not his only focus. He spent time in two important areas. First, he spent time in solitude with the Father. Second, he spent large amounts of time with the 12.

Most contemporary ministry leaders face these same issues. While it is important to spend time with the Father and invest in the 12, we are pressed by the needs of the multitude.

First, he spent time in solitude with the Father.
Second, he spent large amounts of time with the 12.

The Strategic Investment in the 12

Across the Gospels, we see Jesus spending time investing in the 12. He lived with them, talked with them, taught important truths to them, and had them practice these truths. To advance God's kingdom work in our ministry and around the world, we need to do what Jesus did and invest in emerging leaders.

I like the simple strategy John Mark Comer puts forth in his book *Practicing the Way: Be With Jesus. Become Like Him. Do As He Did.* These 10 simple words say so much:

- Be with Jesus.
- Become like him.
- Do as he did.

To advance God's kingdom work in our ministry and around the world, we need to do what Jesus did and invest in emerging leaders.

One way to do a quick assessment is to look at time spent in these five areas:

1. Time with the Lord.
2. Time with your family.
3. Time with the 12 in your world.
4. Time with the multitude.
5. Time with ministry machinery.

For full-time ministry leaders, these five areas make up most of your non-sleeping hours and all of your vocational ministry hours. What do you learn from this quick assessment?

This past year, I was coaching an experienced pastor. He began to realize that nearly all of his ministry hours focused on preparing sermons and doing administrative work at his desk. This is almost entirely ministry to the multitude and accompanying ministry machinery.

Leaders Are Hand-Crafted, Not Mass Produced.

Jesus often taught the multitude in **large groups** through preaching-type events. However, when it came to developing leaders, Jesus did so primarily in **small groups** and **one-on-one**. These three different settings are all important. While good things can happen in large and small groups, there are important leadership development issues that can only be addressed one-on-one. We can see in the ministry of Jesus and in everyday life that leaders are hand-crafted, not mass produced.

We can see in the ministry of Jesus and in everyday life that leaders are hand-crafted, not mass produced.

How Should We Pick the 12?

In earlier sections, we discussed ministry to the multitude and investing in the 12. The next question is, "Who are my 12?" First, it doesn't have to be 12. It could be 5, 10, or even 15 depending on your bandwidth and capacity.

When deciding on who you should invest in, here are some principles to consider. Some of these principles are in the spiritual realm while others are in the natural realm, In the **spiritual** realm like Jesus, we want to **start with prayer,** as we read in Luke 6:12-13:

One of those days Jesus went out to a mountainside to pray and spent the night praying to God. When morning came, he called his disciples to him and chose twelve of them.

From this text, we can see that Jesus spent time in solitude before deciding on the 12. Spiritually, we can do the same thing. I suggest spending some time in solitude asking God who you might focus on going forward. Remember that this is not a perfect process. Even Jesus had Judas. If you lean into some relationships that don't quite pan out, don't lose heart.

Some of these principles are in the spiritual realm and some are in the natural realm.

Who is the Lord showing you that you should invest in? In deciding who will be part of your 12, there are also some issues in the **natural** realm to consider.

- **Interest**: Does the person have interest in growing and leading?
- **Aptitude**: Does the person seem to have the aptitude to lead others well?
- **Bandwidth**: Is the person willing to make room in their lives for their leadership development? There are good people who just aren't willing to take the necessary time.
- **Capacity**: Does that person have the capacity to lead well at the next level?
- **Chemistry**: Does this person care about what you have to say? If they don't, don't take it personally. We just don't click with everyone.

- **Seeking You Out**: Some people will seek you out for mentoring or coaching. While this doesn't mean you have to take on everyone who comes your way, it can be a consideration.
- **Sacrifice and Suffering**: Leadership capacity is built through sacrifice and suffering. The people you invest in need to be willing to make some sacrifices to grow and develop.

Who will make up your 12 can also depend on your role. Here are some examples:

- If you are a parent, part of your 12 could be your children.
- If you are a small group leader, part of your 12 could be the people in your group.
- If you are a youth pastor, your 12 could include a mix of teens and adult volunteers.
- If you are a lead pastor, some of your 12 could be paid staff.
- For some of you, your 12 will be a mix of these different groups.

Extending CPR

In the first half of this book, we discussed how we can bless more people more by caring, praying, and reaching out. This simple approach can be done with those in your world including neighbors, co-workers, friends, family, and those at your church.

We can use the same CPR framework to develop people and leaders by extending caring, praying, and reaching out. We call this CPR$^+$. In brief, this is how CPR$^+$ works:

Caring$^+$: We can only hand-craft leaders if we know them well. Moreover, leadership development happens best in an environment of trust. When we take more time to ask good questions and listen well, we build deeper understanding and trust.

> *We can only hand-craft leaders*
> *if we know them well.*

Praying+: When we take the time to get to know someone better, we are better able to pray for them. We can not only pray for them personally, but we can also better pray for their leadership development journey.

Reaching Out+: With CPR+, we are not just reaching out to see how people are doing: we are reaching out to help the person grow and be stretched in their leadership development journey.

When we care, pray, and reach out at deeper levels, we can **accelerate** peoples' leadership development journey. Let's now unpack these principles in greater detail.

> *When we care, pray, and reach out at deeper levels,*
> *we can **accelerate** peoples' leadership development*
> *journey.*

Coaching Others Well

Coaching is an important part of developing people and leaders. Each year, I have the opportunity of doing over 100 coaching sessions. I also teach coaching courses for doctoral students. I start by telling my students to remember the following key principles:

First, to be a good coach, you need these three foundations:

- Be **caring**. This is the starting point.
- Be **confidential**. What is said needs to stay confidential.
- Be **competent.** You want to coach skillfully. This takes equipping and practice.

Second, to be a competent coach, start with these two things:

- Ask good questions.
- Listen well.

Sure, there are many other things we could add here, but these five foundational elements will get you up and going with your basic coaching skills. Don't be too hard on yourself. If you do these well, you can bless more people more and develop leaders. With additional equipping and practice, you will get even better.

For more material on coaching, I refer you to my book, *Coaching: The First Five Tools for Strategic Leaders*. This and other ClarionStrategy books are listed in the reference section at the end of this book and can be found on Amazon.

Case Study with Chris

The starting point is deciding who will be on your list of 12. Again, this doesn't have to include 12 people. It can be 5, 10, or 15 people long.

Let's say that Chris is in your small group and has shown interest in continued growth. They seem to have the needed interest, aptitude, and bandwidth to lead others. If Chris seems like a fit at this point, you can schedule a time for Caring+, which will be discussed in the next chapter. Here, you can put Chris on your list of 12.

Application for Individuals

1. How much are you currently investing in emerging leaders? If your answer is slim to none, you're in the right place.
2. Brainstorm a list of people who might be candidates.
3. Who is the Lord bringing to mind?

Application for Small Groups

1. How new is all of this for you?

2. What have you learned from some of your past experiences in developing others?

3. How much time and interest do you have for investing in others?

4. At this point, how comfortable do you feel sitting down with people, asking good questions, and listening well?

CARING⁺

*We cared for you because we loved you so much,
we were delighted to share with you not only the
gospel of God but our lives as well.*

–I Thessalonians 2:8

Caring begins with our shared humanity and God's love for all people. CPR⁺ takes caring to the next level as we care for emerging leaders. As mentioned above, these emerging leaders could be those with whom you live, work, or attend church.

WHY IT MATTERS

If we are going to develop people and raise up the needed kingdom leaders for all that needs to be done in our world, we need to start by caring for these potential leaders, emerging leaders, and established leaders. Leading can be hard and lonely work. Most people aren't aware of this reality. As a person moves from a junior leadership role to a senior leadership role, the journey can get even lonelier.

If you want to look at an example of an important person who cared well for others, just look at the life of Barnabas in the Book of Acts. His real name was Joseph of Cyprus, but his nickname was Barnabas, which means Son of Encouragement (Acts 4:36). You too can be that encourager to others.

NOTE: Caring⁺ works at home, at church, and even in your workplace. Employees, particularly those under 40, are looking for supervisors who care about them as people and are committed to their development. CPR⁺ can do just that.

HOW IT WORKS

Caring for others is not complicated. It starts with hoping for the best for others and is extended through on-going intentionality. Caring⁺ goes deeper by seeking to understand a person's background, personality, motivation, and hopes for the future.

Listening to Their Story

Using general CPR, we care for people as best we can, even if we don't know much about them. With CPR⁺, we try to sit down for an hour or so and listen to people's stories. If you have a good memory, you can just listen. I generally ask them if I can take a few notes.

Few things are more precious than a person's story. Our stories form who we are today. Try to listen carefully, praying for them as you go that God will bring out the details that matter most.

Few things are more precious
than a person's story.

When I do CPR⁺ training with experienced ministry leaders, they are often surprised here. They will tell me that they thought they knew the people in their world pretty well. They go on to say how much they gained by going deeper into people's stories.

How to Know a Person

David Brooks, a writer for *The New York Times*, addressed this topic in his 2023 best-selling book, *How to Know a Person: The Art of Seeing Others Deeply and Being Deeply Seen.* Jenn Rizzoto (2023) in her review of Brooks' book writes:

> A practical, heartfelt guide to the art of truly knowing another person in order to foster deeper connections at home, at work, and throughout our lives—from the #1 *New York Times* bestselling author of *The Road to Character* and *The Second Mountain.*

> As David Brooks observes, "There is one skill that lies at the heart of any healthy person, family, school, community organization, or society: the ability to see someone else deeply and make them feel seen—to accurately know another person, to let them feel valued, heard, and understood."

> And yet we humans don't do this well. All around us are people who feel invisible, unseen, misunderstood. The act of seeing another person, Brooks argues, is profoundly creative: How can we look somebody in the eye and see something large in them, and in turn, see something larger in ourselves?

What I like about what Brooks emphasizes here is how connecting with the story of others is enriching for them and us. It forms and deepens relationships in new ways.

Where Would You Like to Be in 5 Years?

Once I have heard a person's thorough and detailed story, I like to ask them, "Where would you like to be in 5 years?" How they answer that question tells you a lot about their hopes and dreams. Here are some different kinds of answers:

- I want to stop working and retire.
- I want to get married.
- I want to get my master's degree.
- I want to go deeper in my relationship with God.
- I want to move to Denver.
- I want to grow in my ministry impact.
- I have no idea.

In much of my coaching and consulting, I ask the question, "Where do you want to go and how can I help?" We want to join in as best we can with people's stories and see how we can best support them going forward. Unless their answer is really odd (They want to be a drug dealer or an international spy), we want to voice our support as they move forward. Note that in some cases, a person may be at a loss as to what to say. Some people just don't think much about the future. If this happens, just go with the flow and see what unfolds in following conversations.

We want to join in as best we can with people's stories and see how we can best support them going forward.

If they say that they want to grow in their relationship with God or in the influence they can have in the lives of others, it may be a good time to introduce Barnabas as a model to encourage them forward.

The Example of Barnabas

Most people don't know who Barnabas is in the Bible. He shows up at the end of Acts chapter 4. In 4:36 and 37, we read these words:

Joseph, a Levite from Cyprus, whom the apostles called Barnabas (which means "son of encouragement"), sold a field he owned and brought the money and put it at the apostles' feet.

He Was Encouraging and Generous

The first thing we read about Barnabas is that his name was Joseph. His nickname was Barnabas, which means that he was an encourager. Next, we learn that he sold a piece of property and gave it to the ministry. We can see here that Barnabas was not only an encourager, he was also generous. How would you describe yourself? To do CPR and CPR+ well, you need to be both encouraging and generous. Caring and investing in the people around us requires an investment of time, effort, and intentionality. Take a few moments to do some self-assessment. Are you encouraging and generous? Ask some of your friends and family members. Then, ask the Lord to give you an encouraging and generous heart.

To do CPR and CPR+ well, we need to be both encouraging and generous.

He Had Eyes of Faith

We next read about Barnabas in Acts Chapter 9:26-27:

When he (Saul) came to Jerusalem, he tried to join the disciples, but they were all afraid of him, not believing that he really was a disciple. **BUT Barnabas took him and brought him to the apostles.** He told them how Saul on his journey had seen the Lord and that the Lord had spoken to him, and how in Damascus he had preached fearlessly in the name of Jesus.

First, we saw that Barnabas was encouraging and generous. We see a continuation of this in this passage. While the disciples were fearful of Saul, Barnabas had eyes of faith to see what could be. In fairness to the disciples, Saul had already killed several Christians. Again, Barnabas didn't see what was, he saw what could be.

Barnabas didn't see what was,
he saw what could be.

When we work with our list of 12 emerging leaders, we want to have eyes of faith, seeing not what was, but what could be. For some years, our son, Josh, was a middle school pastor. He said he loved it because he was not looking at who they were, but at who they were becoming.

Caring with eyes of faith can be transformational for you and the emerging leaders with whom you are working. They might be 14, 24, 44, or even 64 years old. We never know what they might be someday.

When I was in college and a young adult, I had several campus and church ministry leaders who cared for me and spent a lot of time with me. Think about this for a moment. I was arrested at 17, became a Christian at 18, was married at 20, and was called to work overseas at 22. How did this happen? Some of the leaders at my college and in my church saw not who I was, but who I could become. They were CPR[+] leaders in my life.

WHAT TO DO NEXT

Like Barnabas, pray that God will give you eyes of faith. Look around and see where God is at work in the lives of people and join in.

Draft a List of Emerging Leader Candidates

As mentioned above, begin by drafting a list of 5, 10, or 15 people. Spend some time in prayer asking the Lord where you should invest your time. You can also look at the natural factors mentioned above. Don't overthink this. First, you will learn more about these relationships as you get up and going. Some may turn out to be more dedicated than you thought, and some may start well but then drop out at some point.

Start Scheduling Some One-on-One Sessions

Once you have drafted your list, you can start scheduling some one-on-one times together. This works well face-to-face, but if distance doesn't allow for such meetings, you can do a Zoom session or phone call.

When people ask why you want to get together, you can simply say that you are trying to get to know people in your church, community, or workplace better.

NOTE: Be sensitive when you are meeting with people of the opposite gender or minors (those under 18). You may want to meet with them on Zoom or with someone else present. I don't meet with teens without permission from their parents.

When You Meet

As you meet with people, be curious and supportive. Ask them to tell you their story over 30-40 minutes. If you are meeting in-person, you can ask them if you can take some notes. I like taking notes so that in the future, I can remember things like where they work, the name of their spouse, and how many children they have.

As you meet with people,
be curious and supportive.

NOTE: I often hear pastors say that they have known a person for some years and thought they knew them pretty well. What they discover, however, is that they often learn a lot of new things about the person and have a better sense as to how they can help them move forward.

In Follow Up

As you close the session, thank them for the time and express your appreciation for the opportunity to hear their story. If your session goes well, you can schedule a future session in a few weeks. If it doesn't seem to go well, you can just thank them for their time and let them know that you enjoyed getting to hear their story.

If your session goes well...
If it doesn't seem to go well...

Case Study with Chris

We mentioned that Chris was in your small group. You ask Chris about getting together for coffee so you can learn more about their life. The time goes well, and Chris shares some things that they would like to move forward in their lives. You let them know that you will be praying for them and that you would like to get together again some time. If it seems right, you can go ahead and schedule your next session.

You are now up and going with Chris and CPR⁺. The goal here is to see if you can help Chris move ahead in their relationship with the Lord and the influence and impact they can have through their leadership. More broadly, your relationship and investment in Chris may help them to have a better marriage, be a better parent, and be more engaged in their workplace.

NOTE: This can be very effective in the workplace without a religious focus. Listening to your employees' stories and helping them to move forward in their development can be life-changing for them.

Application for Individuals

1. Are you naturally an encouraging and generous person? If not, do you want to be?
2. What are some things you want to learn from Jesus and Barnabas?
3. What did you learn as you drafted up your list of 5, 10, or 15 people you could meet with?

Application for Small Groups

1. What stood out to you as we looked at the examples of Jesus and Barnabas?
2. Who are some people you could meet with?
3. How is your schedule and when can you meet with people?
4. Why is it important for men to help women in their leadership development?

NOTE: As you share with others, be sensitive as to confidentiality. You don't have to share the names of the people with whom you talk.

Praying[+]

I keep asking that the God of our Lord Jesus Christ,
the glorious Father, may give you the Spirit of
wisdom and revelation, so that you
may know him better.

–Ephesians 1:17

When you hear someone's story and their hopes for the future, you learn how to better pray for them. When I ask someone where they want to be in five years and they say that they want to grow deeper with the Lord and be used by him in the lives of others, I know how to pray for them.

Why It Matters
Developing emerging leaders for the kingdom harvest is not just a matter of working hard and saying the right things. Developing leaders is a divine adventure as we partner with God to see his work go forward in their lives. I am not here to tell people what to do—I am here to invite them into an adventure with Jesus.

Developing leaders is a divine adventure
as we partner with God to see his work
go forward in their lives.

HOW IT WORKS

Developing leaders is about seeing God's work in people's lives and joining in. Remember Barnabas and Saul from the last chapter. Barnabas was not involved in Saul's conversion on the road to Damascus, but he was instrumental in connecting Saul with the disciples and developing his leadership.

John 17:4: Knowing What Our Work Is

In John 17:4, we read these 15 words of Jesus:

> *I glorified you on earth, having accomplished*
> *the work that you gave me to do.*

Jesus did the things that the Father gave him to do. Before I meet with emerging leaders, I like to pray this prayer: "Lord, there is so much we could talk about; help us to focus on what is most important at this time." I want to do the work that God has for me in that very hour. I want to collaborate with God in this person's growth and development.

"Lord, there is so much we could talk about;
help us to focus on what is most important
at this time."

Real-Time Prayers

When I am talking with an emerging leader, I am also praying at the same time that God will guide the conversation. Sometimes people tear up and may even start crying during a conversation. At this point, I will silently ask the Lord, "Should I go deeper with this or should we move on in the conversation?" As the Lord guides the conversation, more powerful transformation happens.

Follow-Up Prayers

In between conversations, I am praying for the emerging leader. These prayers could be:

- Related to our conversation.
- Other scriptural prayers.
- Something the Lord brings to mind.

Praying for the emerging leaders on your list of 12 helps to support and accelerate their growth and development.

The Divine Adventure

As we emphasized in the earlier section on prayer, this is a divine adventure. We can see God work in a number of supernatural ways through prayer. First, God may bring things to mind for you that you would not otherwise know. When this happens, don't say everything that comes to mind. For example, let's say that the Lord brings to mind that Sue was abused as a child. Instead of saying that to Sue directly, you can ask, "Do you remember experiencing any trauma or abuse when you were younger?" Again, be cautious even when God shows you things that you would not otherwise know. Second, there may be times when the person experiences things that go beyond a natural explanation. For example, let's say the person asks you to pray about a growth on their kidney. Then the next week, the doctor says that their growth is gone. We do believe that healing work can happen supernaturally. Just be cautious about telling people you think they are going to be healed. Sometimes we get it wrong and we don't want to say things that are not helpful.

WHAT TO DO NEXT

Building your skills in praying for emerging leaders takes practice. As time goes by, see if you can build these skills:

- Hearing God's voice for this person.
- Hearing God's voice as you meet with people.
- Learning scriptural prayers you can pray for others.
- Learning to "watch and pray" (Matthew 26:41) at the same time.

Tracking Your Prayers for People

When I talk with people, I usually take notes. Because I work with lots of people, it is too much to just keep it in my head. I then use these notes to pray for the person in between our conversations.

You can keep notes on paper or in a digital format. Some coaches will review the focus of the session so they can more quickly move to that focus at the next session. Some even go so far as to email the coachee a day or two ahead as a reminder.

There is a balance here. You don't want to be so organized that you miss fruitful work on issues that have come up recently. This is where it is important to realize that each person is different. Some people are very structured and move ahead with clarity and focus session after session. Others are more spontaneous and will have issues that come up that they want to discuss.

When a person has a front-burner issue that has just come up that they want to focus on, it is fine to move away from the structured agenda to deal with these topics. If new "front-burner" issues arise at nearly every session, you should voice your concern that perhaps things are too chaotic.

Case Study with Chris

You are now up and going with Chris and CPR⁺. The goal here is to pray to the Lord that Chris would experience the fullness of Christ in their life. Hopefully, Chris is able to consistently move forward, although sometimes people have seasons of rapid growth and then lulls. There is nothing wrong with this pattern.

Application for Individuals

1. What is your current pattern of praying for people around you?

2. Do you have a good memory for how to pray for people or would it be better for you to write down their pray requests?

3. Do you have someone you can check in with each month to keep you on track with praying for others?

Application for Small Groups

1. Who in the group is more comfortable praying for people? How did you develop that comfort level?

2. Break into twos and threes and practice praying for one other. If this is new for you, just listen to others. You can also practice using the prayers in the Appendix at the end of this book.

3. Share with the group some answers to prayers that you have experienced.

REACHING OUT⁺

Then Barnabas went to Tarsus to look for Saul, and when he found him, he brought him to Antioch. So for a whole year Barnabas and Saul met with the church and taught great numbers of people.

–Acts 11:25-26

"Thanks for caring." At the end of our time together, I will often ask the people I am meeting with what was most helpful about our time together. Not every time, but sometimes they will mention that they feel that someone cares about their growth and development. Even some older adults will say this is the first time someone has actively helped them to move forward. Just this week, a man in his 60s told me that he has never had a person who reached out to affirm and develop his leadership. By consistently reaching out to those around you, you can make a big difference in their lives and leadership.

WHY IT MATTERS

Good things can happen in a large group. Even more can happen in a small group. However, some very important things can only happen in a one-on-one setting. As we said earlier, leaders are hand-crafted, not mass-produced. Reaching out for a one-on-one meeting is what Barnabas did with Saul. It is what Jesus did with his disciples. It is what we can do with those around us. We can't do it with a hundred people, but we can do it with 12.

Leaders are hand-crafted, not mass-produced.

HOW IT WORKS

Here are some principles and practices that can help to shape your one-on-one times with those on your list of 12.

Take the Initiative

At the top of this chapter, we read "Barnabas went to Tarsus to look for Saul." If you want to develop emerging leaders, you need to be active, not passive. This is true for the 14-year-old in your family as well as the 30-year-old in your church. Take the initiative to get together.

If you want to develop emerging leaders,
you need to be active, not passive.

At Least Once a Month

I suggest that you meet with your list of 12 at least once a month. If you meet less than this, it is usually difficult to sustain momentum and development. If this feels like too much, just start with 3 or 6 people.

As mentioned earlier, when I work with full-time pastors or ministry leaders, I will sometimes ask them to track their time for the month in these five areas:

1.   Time with family.
2.   Time with the Lord.
3.   Time with the 12.
4.   Time with the multitude.
5.   Time with ministry machinery.

If a pastor works around 150-250 hours per month, a dozen hours to invest in their list of 12 can make a difference in so many areas. We say this because any ministry over 100 people needs a team of people to care, pray, and reach out to those in the congregation and community. Yes, your list of 12 is a good way to start doing CPR with everyone in your church.

Good Coaching and Mentoring Practices

Reaching out to people at the next level is just a matter of putting good coaching and mentoring practices to use. Let's do some quick review:

First, to be a good coach, you need these three foundations:

- Be **caring**. This is the starting point.
- Be **confidential**. What is said needs to stay confidential.
- Be **competent.** You want to coach skillfully. This takes equipping and practice.

Second, to be a competent coach, start with these two things:

- Ask good questions.
- Listen well.

If you look at the Table of Contents of my book *Coaching: The First Five Tools for Strategic Leaders*, you will see these five Cs:

- CONNECTING with Care.
- CLARIFYING the Goal.
- COLLABORATING Creatively with Questions.
- CREATING a Plan Forward.
- CLOSING with Purpose.

You don't have to follow this template strictly but using it even informally can be helpful. Let's look at each element.

- CONNECTING with Care: Start conversations with words of care and affirmation. Ask them about anything that is new in their life since you last met. The key here is to not be in a rush.
- CLARIFYING the Goal: Here I will often ask, "As we meet today, what would be most helpful to discuss?" Down below we will discuss using a shared agenda.
- COLLABORATING Creatively with Questions: This is the heart of the conversation. Let's say the person wants to talk about getting a new job. You could follow-up with questions about their past jobs, their hopes for a new job, and where they are in the process.
- CREATING a Plan Forward: Toward the end of the conversation, you can ask, "What would be some helpful next steps going forward from this conversation?"
- CLOSING with Purpose: This is the off-ramp for the conversation. You can set the date for the next meeting, review their next steps, and then pray for them.

Again, this is just a framework that is good practice in coaching. Mentoring will sometimes be less formal and less structured as you just ask good questions and listen well, providing some suggestions along the way.

Both coaching and mentoring practices can be helpful as you reach out to the emerging leaders around you.

Shared Agenda

In pure coaching, the agenda is with the person, and they set the direction. With a shared agenda, I look to where the person wants to go, but I also lean in a bit on their personal growth and leadership development. It is a balancing act. For example, I am more than happy to help a person find a new job, but I am also hopeful that they can do CPR in the lives of others.

It also depends on whether the person is a paid client or a friend from church. A paid client usually has more say in where the agenda goes. When I meet with a friend at church for free, I am trying to help them to grow personally and professionally as well as equip them to bless more people more and develop others.

The One-Foot Fence

At the end of each session, I am often looking for a one-foot fence that could move them forward. A one-foot fence is something to do that is not large or difficult. For example, if a person wants to become an HR director, we might discuss finding an HR director they could talk with. If a person wants to grow in their prayer lives, we might discuss them praying five minutes a day for a week or two.

A one-foot fence also helps me to understand their desire to move forward. Some people will consistently move past every one-foot fence. Others will rarely make even simple progress. This helps me to understand their interest and commitment to growth.

Zone of Proximal Development

The Zone of Proximal Development was developed by a Russian educator and can be very helpful. ZPD is about not challenging people too much or too little. Research tells us that developing people is like physical therapy. If you under-challenge people, they will under-develop. If you over-challenge people, they will under-develop because they may become stressed, or in the case of physical therapy, they may injure themselves.

The goal is to work toward challenges that are:

- **Developmentally appropriate**: What they need to move forward at this time.
- **Challenging:** Will stretch them to the point they may even be a little nervous.
- **Supportive:** Not overwhelming.
- **Not too basic or static:** They change over time.

I was talking recently with a lay ministry leader I coach. We were talking about adding some people to his ministry team. I asked, "Does this sound exciting or scary?" He said a bit of both. That is probably in the "zone." Like Goldilocks, "Not too hot, not too cold, just right."

Getting Practice

As you reach out to people each month and discuss areas of growth, it is important to emerging leaders to get some practice. For example, let's say that your church provides some training for small group leaders. Once that training is finished, it is important for people to get some practice. That practice should be developmentally appropriate. In other words, it should be at the right level for the person. If they have experience leading, they might start as a new group leader. If leading is newer for them, they could start as a host or assistant leader. Our job as the person doing the CPR$^+$ is to understand the person and then seek out the appropriate context for them to practice at their level.

WHAT TO DO NEXT

You have your list of 12, more or less. You have met with them to hear their stories as well as their hopes for the future. You are praying for them. Now look at meeting with them a time or two each month. The goal is to reach out in a way that fosters their ongoing growth using the principles of:

- Coaching and mentoring
- Shared agenda
- One-foot fence
- Zone of Proximal Development (ZPD)
- Getting practice

It Takes Practice

Just as we want our emerging 12 to get practice, we need to practice as well. When I am training coaches or graduate students, I will say, "In your first 10 sessions, just try not to hurt anyone." When you have 20, 40, or 60 sessions under your belt, you will feel more comfortable and competent. Just be patient with yourself as you get some practice.

Case Study with Chris

You are now up and going with Chris. He is doing CPR consistently and you are meeting each month for CPR+. At some point, you can have Chris begin to do CPR+ with others.

In may help to take notes as you work with Chris and others.

Application for Individuals

1. What experience with coaching and mentoring do you have, if any? How many sessions do you think you have had?
2. What areas of coaching and mentoring would you like to grow in?
3. What are some next steps you can take in this area?
4. Would it help to get a copy of *Coaching: The First Five Tools for Strategic Leaders* on Amazon?

Application for Small Groups

1. Go around the groups or in groups of 2-3 to discuss your experience in this area.
2. How are coaching and mentoring different?
3. Have a couple of people in your group do a reaching out role play session.

CPR⁺ Next Steps

We have now covered both CPR and CPR⁺. The combination of these can help you to both bless people and develop people along the path of your everyday life.

WHY IT MATTERS

Throughout this book, we have emphasized how you can put these skills into practice. These practices are not hard, and you can do it! You may want to find a friend who can do CPR in parallel with you. You can both give it a try and then compare notes on how it is going.

These practices are not hard, and you can do it!

HOW IT WORKS

Review the key concepts for caring⁺, praying⁺, and reaching out⁺. From there, it is a matter of getting started and practicing. You can practice on a friend, someone in your group, or even a family member. Don't be afraid to ask someone if you can practice with them.

WHAT TO DO NEXT

Start with CPR so you can develop your comfort and confidence with the concepts and practices. You can then move on to CPR⁺ with some folks in your world. When it comes to CPR⁺, remember the law of thirds. First, some of the people you meet with will be very excited about doing CPR with others or that you are doing CPR⁺ with them. Second, most people will appreciate your initiative but may not describe it as life-changing. Third, a few people may not notice or care much about what you are doing. In other words, be prepared for the reality that not all people will respond in the same way. People are different and their responses will be different.

Using the ACE Model to Support Development

Every month, I work with MBA students with the goal of helping them become effective managers and leaders. A traditional academic program is not enough. Not only are these programs expensive and time-consuming, but the results don't always translate into developed leaders. The ACE Model can help here. The three elements include:

- Academic Learning (formal and informal)
- Coaching and Community (purposeful relationships)
- Experience in the Field (practicing what you are learning)

We will look at a two-fold CPR⁺ example. Let's say you are doing CPR⁺ with Chris and that you are equipping them to do it with others. First, you can give Chris some informal **academic** instruction. You could have them read some of this book and/or listen to some 8-minute *Multiply Your Leadership* podcasts on these topics (the link for this series can be found in the Reference section at the end of this book). Second, you could **coach** them on how to put CPR into daily practice. Third, they could get some **experience in the field** through regular practice. The ACE Model can be very simple and practical as you do CPR⁺ with others in your church, community, and/or workplace.

Using CPR⁺ at Work

While most of the discussion is this book has focused on working with people in a Christian context, these tools can also work well in many work settings. Here are some thoughts on this from a *Harvard Business Review* article entitled "Leading with Compassion Has Research-Backed Benefits":

Compassion is a vital component of effective leadership. People's brains respond more positively to leaders who show compassion, as demonstrated by neuroimaging research. Creating a compassionate culture has been linked with lower employee emotional exhaustion (one of the elements of burnout) as well as lower employee absenteeism from work.

Recent evidence supports this. Contrary to what many employers currently believe, the recent wave of employee attrition has less to do with economics and more to do with relationships (or lack thereof). The data support that employees' decisions to stay in a job largely come from a sense of belonging, feeling valued by their leaders, and having caring and trusting colleagues. Conversely, employees are more likely to quit when their work relationships are merely transactional. So, how do leaders foster more meaningful relationships in organizations and inspire loyalty? In a word: compassion.

Author Simon Sinek describes that when leaders focus less on being "in charge" and more on taking care of those who are in their charge, that's a sure sign of a compassionate leader. Numerous studies show that when leaders are primarily focused on the well-being of their employees, this is a strong predictor of employee job satisfaction, perceived organizational support, loyalty and trust in the organization, and retention. It also has been linked with improved employee job performance (by boosting employee motivation), and better team performance. (Trzeciak et al., 2023)

Instead of using religious words like prayer, you can just let people know you care and that you were thinking about them.

I saw this in action when I was a professor in China. While the university officials did not have any interest in our Christian ideals, they appreciated the care and concern we demonstrated toward students. Some years ago, a friend was at the Ministry of Education office in Beijing. The office had a whiteboard with a line down the middle. On one side was a list of Christian organizations that sent teachers to China. On the other side was a list of other organizations. The official said to my friend, "We would only hire Christian teachers if we could get enough of them." In this secular, communist country, they didn't always understand our Christian foundations, but they valued the application of CPR on their campuses. Wherever you work, people appreciate it when you care for them, think of them, and actively reach out to them in appropriate ways.

Case Study with Chris

As you begin to meet with Chris each month, you have the privilege of joining with them on their journey of growth and development. This journey will have several layers:

- **CPR with Chris**: You can begin by doing CPR with Chris.
- **Chris doing CPR with others**: You can then move to the place where Chris does CPR with people in their world.
- **Doing CPR+ with Chris**: Next, you can do CPR+ with Chris as you invest in their growth and development.
- **Chris can do CPR+ with others**: Lastly, Chris can do CPR+ with people around them.

For more on sustaining CPR and CPR+ with others, take a look at Appendix A, "Four Generations of Sustainable CPR/CPR+."

Application for Individuals

1. In which area of CPR+ do you feel the strongest?
2. In which area of CPR+ do you feel the weakest? You might want to go back and reread that section and then practice with a friend.
3. What are some next steps you can take in this area?

Application for Small Groups

1. Have a couple of people in your group do a short role play with CPR$^+$.
2. Discuss any questions you might have concerning any aspects of CPR$^+$ with the group.
3. You can break into pairs and practice going both ways.

CPR⁺ LEADER LIST OF 12

Throughout this book, we have talked about your list of 12. As mentioned, this list could be 5, 10, or 15 people long. Next, this is not a static list. One of the reasons we don't have a place in this book for you to write the names is that the list will change.

Over time, people will come onto and off your list. You may add people to your list as you move from 5 names to 10 names. People will come off your list as they develop and become more independent.

I often say that I don't coach people forever. There is often a season of focused growth and development and then a new season begins. Our goal is for people to get to a place where they can direct their own path forward and can invest in others themselves.

APPENDIX A:

Four Generations of Sustainable CPR/CPR⁺

To keep a movement sustainable, we need a sustainable plan. In 2 Timothy 2:2, we see a pattern for ministry multiplication:

> And the things you have heard me say in the presence of many witnesses entrust to reliable people who will also be qualified to teach others.

In this passage, we can see the four generations:

- **Paul** is the author here.
- He is writing to **Timothy.**
- Timothy should entrust these things to **reliable people.**
- Who will then teach **others.**

Paul (1st Generation): CPR/CPR⁺ Coach

Think of your CPR and CPR⁺ trainer or teacher as the first generation. If it works, this can be a person who can keep you engaged and moving ahead. If not, look for someone else who can keep you motivated and accountable. Think of this person as your CPR/CPR⁺ coach or encourager.

Timothy (2nd Generation): CPR/CPR⁺ Leader

This is you. You have learned and are using CPR. Now you are charged with passing it on to others in two ways. First, you want to do CPR yourself. Second, you can pass this simple tool onto others. You can then move on to CPR⁺ as you invest in others.

Reliable People (3rd Generation): CPR/CPR+ Practitioner

You can now pass on what you have learned in the way of CPR and CPR+ to others by becoming their coach or encourager.

Others (4th Generation): CPR/CPR+ Apprentices

Encourage those you have equipped to bless others and invest in them using these simple tools. You may never know how many people you have touched.

APPENDIX B:

Scriptural Prayers

The Bible is filled with Scriptures that can be used to pray for those around you.

Prayers for Christians: "We pray…"

- Colossians 1:9 (NIV) [that you may be filled] with the knowledge of his will through all the wisdom and understanding that the Spirit gives.
- James 5:16 [that you can] confess your sins to each other and pray for each other so that you may be healed.
- 1 Peter 3:15 [that you will] always be prepared to give an answer to everyone who asks you to give the reason for the hope that you have. But do this with gentleness and respect.
- Romans 15:31 that the God of hope fill you with all joy and peace as you trust in him, so that you may overflow with hope by the power of the Holy Spirit.
- Ephesians 1:17-18 [that] the God of our Lord Jesus Christ, the glorious Father, may give you the Spirit of wisdom and revelation, so that you may know him better. I pray also that the eyes of your heart may be enlightened in order that you may know the hope to which he has called you, the riches of his glorious inheritance in the saints, and his incomparably great power for us who believe.
- Ephesians 3:16-19 [that] out of his glorious riches he may strengthen you with power through his Spirit in your inner being, so that Christ may dwell in your hearts through faith. And I pray that you, being rooted and established in

love, may have power, together with all the saints, to grasp how wide and long and high and deep is the love of Christ, and to know this love that surpasses knowledge – that you may be filled to the measure of all the fullness of God.

- Philippians 1:9-12 [that] your love may abound more and more in knowledge and depth of insight, so that you may be able to discern what is best and may be pure and blameless until the day of Christ, filled with the fruit of righteousness that comes through Jesus Christ – to the glory and praise of God.

- 1 Thessalonians 3:12-13 [that] the Lord [will] make your love increase and overflow for each other and for everyone else . . . May he strengthen your hearts so that you will be blameless and holy in the presence of our God and Father when our Lord Jesus comes with all his holy ones.

- 2 Thessalonians 1:11-12 that our God may count you worthy of his calling, and that by his power he may fulfill every good purpose of yours and every act prompted by your faith. We pray this so that the name of our Lord Jesus may be glorified in you, and you in him, according to the grace of our God and the Lord Jesus Christ.

Prayers for Those Who Have Yet to Meet Christ: "We pray…"

- 2 Corinthians 4:4 that they [can] see the light of the gospel that displays the glory of Christ, who is the image of God.

- 1 John 1:9 [that they might know that] if we confess our sins, he is faithful and just to forgive us our sins and to cleanse us from all unrighteousness.

- Psalm 119:18 [that you will] open [their] eyes to see the wonderful truths in your instructions.

- Acts 26:18 [that God will] open their eyes, so that they may turn from darkness to light and from the power of Satan to

God, that they may receive forgiveness of sins and a place among those who are sanctified by faith in me.

- Ephesians 1:18 that the eyes of your heart may be enlightened in order that you may know the hope to which he has called you.

Appendix C:
CPR Friends List

NOTE: You can copy the following two pages onto one 8.5 x 11 sheet.

	J	F	M	A	M	J	J	A	S	O	N	D
Name												
P												
R												
Prayer												
Name												
P												
R												
Prayer												
Name												
P												
R												
Prayer												
Name												
P												
R												
Prayer												
Name												
P												
R												
Prayer												
Name												
P												
R												
Prayer												
Name												
P												
R												
Prayer												

		J	F	M	A	M	J	J	A	S	O	N	D
Name	P												
	R												
Prayer													
Name	P												
	R												
Prayer													
Name	P												
	R												
Prayer													
Name	P												
	R												
Prayer													
Name	P												
	R												
Prayer													
Name	P												
	R												
Prayer													
Name	P												
	R												
Prayer													
Name	P												
	R												
Prayer													

Appendix D:
Leading a CPR Small Group

CPR and CPR⁺ are both well-suited for a small group setting. There are two levels where CPR and CPR⁺ could be used. First, simple CPR and CPR⁺ could be used in every small group. In other words, a leader can do CPR and CPR⁺ with the people in the group. For example, you could have a small group that is studying the Book of Ephesians and the leader could do CPR and CPR⁺ with the participants.

The leader could do CPR and CPR⁺
with the people in the group.

Second, you could have a CPR-focused group. A CPR-focused group is one in which CPR and CPR⁺ are studied and lived out each week. The group might use this book for 8-15 weeks and go through a chapter each week, practicing along the way.

A CPR-focused group is one in which
CPR and CPR⁺ are studied
and lived out each week.

Here are several processes that can help a CPR-focused group go well.

- **Securing support from your small group leadership team:** Start by taking the idea to your small group pastor or ministry leaders to see if they would support using CPR in a small group or creating a CPR-focused group.
- **Putting your CPR Small Group leadership team together:** Ideally, your group has a leader (single or couple), assistant leader (single or couple), and a host (single or couple).
- **Deciding on your format:** How many weeks will you meet and when will you start and end?
- **Marketing your upcoming group to others:** Share with others the value being in this group can bring. This works best if you start letting people know about the upcoming group a month or two ahead of time.
- **Getting ready for your first meeting:** Get copies of this book for each person in your group with time to spare. You can go to Amazon to get the book for $5.99 each (not including shipping) or if you have a month of lead time, you can order them in bulk for $5.00 a copy (includes shipping / minimum of 10) by contacting me at Info@ClarionLife.org.
- **Your first meeting:** Who is going to do what? What is your schedule for your time together?
- **Following meetings:** Are you modeling CPR by touching base with the people outside the group each month?
- **Ending well:** How can you provide some follow-up support and accountability?
- **Sustaining a CPR movement:** Can you continue with another CPR group or CPR$^+$ group in the weeks or months ahead?

Appendix E:

CPR and Your Local Church

CPR can help your church bless those in your congregation and your community. Below are several phases you can consider as a church. Each phase puts you at a better level of caring for the people around you.

Phase 1: CPR for the Church

- **Sunday Sermon**: A simple place to start is by sharing CPR in a simple Sunday sermon. This will let everyone know how they can get started with CPR in their world.
- **Equipping Workshop**: You can also do a workshop on equipping people to integrate CPR into their life and work.

Phase 2: CPR and Life Groups

A great way to start caring for those in your church is by integrating CPR into your life groups or small groups. You can do this in several ways. If you equip your group leaders to do CPR with the people in their groups and half of your people are in groups, then you are well on your way to providing pastoral care for those in your church.

- **Life Group Leaders**: When you do your training for group leaders, you can ask them to do CPR with those who attend their groups. This is a natural process, as your group leaders probably already know the names of the people in their group. Then, it is just a matter of having them pray for the people in their group. Lastly, you can encourage leaders to touch base with the people in their group each month outside of the group meeting.

- **Those Who Attend Life Groups**: Once CPR is working well for the group through the group leader, the leader can go over CPR with the people in the group. Attendees can be encouraged to identify a few people in their world with whom they can do CPR.
- **Youth Ministry**: CPR can also be used in youth ministries. You can equip both youth leaders and teens to use CPR with those in the church and those in the community.

Phase 3: CPR for the Entire Congregation

If you are integrating CPR into your life groups, it is not difficult for a care team to extend pastoral care to the entire congregation.

- **Church Roster:** Many churches use a software platform and therefore have a list of all the adults and teens in the church. See if you can note in your database which people are in life groups or some kind of small group. If CPR is happening at the group level, you should then be able to generate a list of people who are not in a group. This list can go to your care team.
- **Care Team:** Let's say that there are seven people on a care team, and you have 70 people on your church roster who are not already in some kind of small group. You can divide up those 70 people and create a list of 10 people for each person on your care team. If this care team can do CPR with these, you now have a pastoral care net for everyone who considers your church their church home.

Phase 4: CPR for Visitors

If you really want to take your pastoral care to the next level, you can extend CPR to even include visitors.

- **Outreach or Visitation Team:** When people let you know that they have visited your church and have provided you with some type of contact information, you can pass this on to the visitation team. The visitation team member can contact the person and let them know that they are going to be praying for the person until they find a church home, even if it is not your church. This is a way you can connect and bless those who visit your church in a meaningful way that does not aggressively recruit them.

Phase 5: CPR for the Community

- **Those You Know:** As CPR becomes commonplace with people in your church, you can encourage them to bless not only other people in your church, but also people they know in the community.
- **Those You Meet:** When you are out in the community, you will often meet people you can bless through CPR. Take the cashier you see regularly at your favorite grocery store. On a slower day at the store, you can ask that person how you could pray for them. You can then reach out to them each month as you see them at the store. In this way, you can bless people in our lonely world. You can use these same practices at a restaurant.

APPENDIX F:

How I Found New Life in Christ

You could say that I am a product of CPR. A girl at my high school invited me to attend her church. I said, "No, no, no." I did not grow up going to church and did not have any interest. Well, she kept asking. I wasn't interested in church, but I *was* interested in her and so I eventually said, "Yes."

That Sunday rolled around, and I found myself in a Baptist church in Dayton, Ohio. As the pastor gave his message, he talked about how we could find forgiveness for our sins and new life in Christ.

I thought to myself, "These nice church people don't have many sins to be forgiven, but I have truckloads of sin in my life." When the invitation came, I followed a simple process that many churches use.

Admit
When the pastor gave the invitation to come forward, I quickly went forward. I admitted that I had sinned and fallen short of what God had for me. Walking forward during a church service is not the key here. The key is recognizing that we have fallen short of what God has for us. (Romans 3:23, Romans 6:23, Romans 5:8)

Believe
Second, based on what the Bible says, I believed that Jesus is the Son of God and that he came and died on the cross that my sins might be forgiven. (Romans 8:1)

Confess

Lastly, I confessed my sins and that I wanted to accept Jesus and his work for my salvation. It would be a while before I fully understood that I was a new person in Christ. However, that day, I put my faith in Christ and committed to follow him going forward. (Romans 10:9, 13, John 3:16)

This process gives you the basics, but there is so much more to living out our new life in Christ. A great place to start is by reading through the Book of John. Below are some helpful verses.

Verses From the Book of John

The following verses are found in chapter 3 of the Book (also called the Gospel) of John:

> 3:3 Jesus replied, "Very truly I tell you, no one can see the kingdom of God unless they are born again."

> 3: 5-7 Jesus answered, "Very truly I tell you, no one can enter the kingdom of God unless they are born of water and the Spirit. Flesh gives birth to flesh, but the Spirit gives birth to spirit. You should not be surprised at my saying, 'You must be born again.'"

> 3:14-15 "so the Son of Man must be lifted up, that everyone who believes may have eternal life in him."

> 3:16 "For God so loved the world that he gave his one and only Son, that whoever believes in him shall not perish but have eternal life."

You too can make the life-changing decision to follow Jesus. Since I put my faith in Jesus decades ago, I have been blessed beyond measure. Sure, I needed lots of ongoing healing and growth, especially to find freedom from my tough upbringing. Through these many years, God has been faithful in walking with me on this journey.

If you have made the decision to follow Jesus, I would love to hear from you. Feel free to email me at Info@ClarionLife.org or Rick@CPDistrict.org

Resources

Here are some resources you can use with the material found here:

Books

- **ClarionStrategy Series**
    - *Strategic Leaders Are Made, Not Born*: *The First Five Tools for Escaping the Tactical Tsunami* by Rick Mann
    - *Building Strategic Organizations*: *The First Five Tools for Strategy and Strategic Planning* by Rick Mann
    - *Strategic Finance*: *The First Five Tools for Strategic Leaders* by Rick Mann and David Tarrant
    - *Coaching*: *The First Five Tools for Strategic Leaders* by Rick Mann
    - *Enterprise Leadership*: *The First Five FIELD Tools* by Rick Mann and Dean Diehl
    - *Nonprofit Leadership and Management*: *A Toolbox for Moving from Surviving to Thriving* by Rick Mann and Jeremy Mann

- **ClarionLife Series**
    - *Living and Leading Intentionally*: *31 Tools for Becoming Christ-centered, Spirit-filled, Healthy, Strategic Leaders* by Rick Mann and Rob Douglas (coming in late 2024)
    - *Becoming Multiplying Ministry Leaders Who Multiply Leaders*: *Lessons from Jesus, Barnabas, and Paul* by Rick Mann (coming in late 2024)

- **Podcast Series by Rick Mann**
  - *Multiply Your Leadership*
    8-minute episodes on ministry leadership
    https://sites.libsyn.com/478650/site
  - *Future Proof Your Strategic Leadership*
    8-minute episodes on marketplace leadership
    https://sites.libsyn.com/316355/site

About the Author

Rick has served in a number of leadership roles across a wide variety of industries. He currently serves as Professor of Leadership and Strategy as well as Program Director for the MBA and DBA programs at Trevecca Nazarene University. He also currently serves as the part-time Director of Leadership Development for the Central Pacific District of the Christian and Missionary Alliance.

In the past, he has served as the President of Crown College (MN), a program director in China, an executive coach, and coaching trainer.

His mission is to coach and multiply leaders one STEP at a time. STEP stands for 1) Starting things, 2) Teaching things, 3) Equipping people, and 4) Pastoring people.

Rick has an MDiv from Ambrose University (Canada), an MBA from the University of Minnesota, and an MA and PhD from Ohio State University. He is also an Associate Certified Coach through the International Coach Federation (ICF).

Rick and Cheri are partners in ministry, having worked overseas together, pastored together, and now work with ministry leaders together. Cheri is a nurse practitioner by training. Her primary ministry gifting is in intercession. They have three married sons, and yes, 14 grandchildren.

References

Brooks, David. (2023). *How to Know a Person: The Art of Seeing Others Deeply and Being Deeply Seen*. Random House.

Comer, J.M. (2024). *Practicing the Way: Be with Jesus. Become like him. Do as he did.* Waterbrook.

Damiani, A. (September 11, 2023). Take a Risk and Make a Friend. *Christianity Today*.

Earley, J. W. (2023). *Made for People: Why We Drift into Loneliness and How to Fight for a Life of Friendship*. Zondervan.

Johnson, D. (2021). *Experiencing the Trinity: Living in the Relationship at the Centre of the Universe*. Canadian Church Leaders Network; 2nd ed.

Weissbourd, R., Batanova, M., Lovison, V., and Torres, E. (2021). *Loneliness in America: How the Pandemic Has Deepened an Epidemic of Loneliness and What We Can Do About It*. Harvard

Mann, R. (2019). Coaching: *The First Five Tools for Strategic Leaders*. ClarionStrategy.

Nobel, J. (2023). *Project Unlonely: Healing Our Crisis of Disconnection*. Avery.

Reimer, R. (2020). *Spiritual Authority*. Renewal International Ministries.

Renken, E. (January 23, 2020). Most Americans Are Lonely, And Our Workplace Culture May Not Be Helping. *NPR*.

Rizzoto, J. (2023). How to Know a Person, by Jenn. *The Book Review Crew*. https://thebookreviewcrew.com/how-to-know-a-person-a-review-by-jenn/

Sinek, Simon (2011). *Start with Why*. Portfolio.

Trzeciak, S., Mazzarelli, A., & Seppälä, E. (2023). Leading with Compassion Has Research-Backed Benefits. *Harvard Business Review*. https://hbr.org/2023/02/leading-with-compassion-has-research-backed-benefits

Made in USA - Kendallville, IN
10135_9781737320357
06 03 2025 2245